HELP ME —
I'M DISCOURAGED!

HELP ME —
I'M DISCOURAGED!

Overcoming Emotional Battles
With the Power of God's Word

by

Joyce Meyer

Harrison House
Tulsa, Oklahoma

2nd Printing

HELP ME — I'M DISCOURAGED!
Overcoming Emotional Battles
With the Power of God's Word
ISBN 1-57794-013-X
Copyright © 1998 by Joyce Meyer
Life In The Word, Inc.
P. O. Box 655
Fenton, Missouri 63026

Published by Harrison House, Inc.
P. O. Box 35035
Tulsa, Oklahoma 74153

Contents

Introduction

꧁꧂

We have all been disappointed at one time or another. In fact, it would be surprising if we went through the week without encountering some kind of disappointment. We are "appointed" (set in a certain direction) for something to happen a certain way, and when it doesn't happen that way, we become "dis-appointed."

Disappointment not dealt with turns into discouragement. If we stay discouraged very long, we are liable to become devastated, and devastation leaves us unable to handle anything.

Many devastated Christians are lying along the roadside of life because they have not learned how to handle disappointment. The devastation they are experiencing now most likely began with a minor disappointment not dealt with.

Jesus healed all who were oppressed of the devil. (Acts 10:38 KJV.) It is not God's will for us to live disappointed, devastated or oppressed! When we become "disappointed," we must learn to become "re-appointed" to keep from becoming discouraged, then devastated.

When we learn to place our hope and confidence in Jesus the Rock (1 Corinthians 10:4) and resist the devil at the onset, we can live in the joy and peace of the Lord, free from discouragement.

Part 1

Free From Oppression

1

≈

The Greater One Lives in Us

...God anointed and consecrated
Jesus of Nazareth with the [Holy]
Spirit and with strength and ability
and power;...He went about doing
good and, in particular, curing all
who were harassed and oppressed
by [the power of] the devil, for God
was with Him.

Acts 10:38

During His earthly ministry, Jesus' calling, we could even say "His job," was to go
about in the anointing of the Holy Spirit
upon Him and deliver all those who were
oppressed by the devil. That power is available to us today. It is not God's will for His
children to be harassed or oppressed, and

Jesus' power is available to deliver us from oppression today.

According to Webster's dictionary,[1] to oppress is "to weigh heavily upon," especially "so as to depress the mind or spirits." Other meanings are "to crush or overwhelm," to press down.

I believe the enemy, Satan, can oppress not only our mind or spirit but any part of our being, including our body and soul. Sometimes he does so without our even knowing what specifically is bothering us.

At times each of us has had something weigh heavily upon us. Most of us have experienced oppression to the point of it being hard to think and make decisions. At other times we have been oppressed physically.

We must keep in mind that Satan at various times will try to oppress different parts of our being in different ways for different reasons. We have the power available to us through Jesus to be aggressive against the devil. If we aren't aggressive toward him, he will be aggressive toward us.

Although the devil is the root of all evil, there are things we do in the flesh that can cause us to feel overwhelmed or bring a heaviness on us. We can feel overwhelmed by not dealing with little problems as they occur. People who gossip, complain, backbite and judge can experience a feeling of heaviness.

In order for us to feel uplifted, as though there were a spring of living water flowing out of us, we must resist the devil who tries to oppress us and all his ways. But we must also refuse to bring oppression and depression upon ourselves. And most important, we must aggressively tackle the things God tells us to do. When we obey God, we will undertake some challenging projects. But the Lord gives us His Spirit to powerfully work in us to enable us to do what He has asked.

Again according to Webster,[2] to be aggressive is to initiate forceful action, to be

"energetic" or "boldly assertive" —"enterprising," which itself means to be imaginative.

As it was originally created by God, the
power of man to imagine is not meant to be
some kind of wicked, evil thing. It is the creative imagination of man that keeps coming
up with new ideas and bringing forth new
processes through innovative thoughts.
Think how creative Adam must have been to
name all the animals in his holy state before
he fell into sin. Some of us have trouble
coming up with a name for our dog!

Led by the Spirit

By following the leading of the Holy
Spirit and allowing the fruit of the Spirit
(Galatians 5:22,23) to be evident in our lives,
we are initiators and innovators. We can pur-
posefully bring forth the creative ability of
God that is on the inside of us. Many people
are bored because they are in an "oppressed"
state rather than in a "godly aggressive"

state. Exercising our God-given creativity eliminates boredom!

Some of us are naturally more creative, imaginative, innovative and aggressive than others. But each of us can use the creativity, imagination, innovativeness and aggression that God has placed within us to make our lives more satisfying, productive and fulfilling.

Instead of waiting for something to come on us, we can initiate. For example, instead of waiting for others to be friendly toward us, we can initiate friendships.

Keep the Devil on the Run

The devil lies to us. (John 8:44.) If we aren't aggressive against him and stop listening to his lies, he will run our life. He goes about *like* a roaring lion (1 Peter 5:8), but we *have* the Lion of Judah, Jesus, *inside* us. *We* are the ones who should be doing the roaring!

When the devil makes one move toward us, we should keep ourselves so spiritually attuned that we pick up exactly what he's trying to do and back him down. It should take only a few seconds.

The devil is always trying to come against us. As long as we back down, he keeps on coming. If we make one move against him in the authority Jesus made available to us, the devil has to back down.

We need to continue standing in our authority against him. If we stop, he will start moving against us, backing *us* up. The devil is a liar, a bully, a bluff, a deceiver. He comes *like* a lion, but he is not the lion. We believers in Jesus Christ have the power of the greater one on the inside of us. "...greater is he that is in you, than he that is in the world" (1 John 4:4 KJV).

Know the Word well enough that the minute a thought comes into your head that doesn't line up with God's Word, you can say to the devil, "*Liar!* No, I'm not listening to you."

You can spend your life backing up and hiding from the devil, or forcing him to back up.

Choose Life

I call heaven and earth to witness this day against you that I have set before you life and death, the blessings and the curses; therefore choose life, that you and your descendants may live.

Deuteronomy 30:19

Happiness and joy do not come from the outside. They come from within. They are a conscious decision, a deliberate choice, one that we make ourselves each day we live.

In our ministry we have a young woman working for us who has many things she would like to see changed in her life. But despite those challenges, she is happy and joyous.

This young woman is filled with happiness and joy not because she doesn't have any problems but because of the decision she has made to enjoy her life and work in the midst of adversity.

Every day she has a choice: to be filled with misery or to be filled with the joy of the Lord.

That is the same choice that each of us faces every day of our life.

Either we choose to passively listen to the devil and allow him to ruin our life and make us miserable, or we choose to aggressively withstand him so we can live in the fullness of life God has provided for us through His Son Jesus Christ.

Either way we will still get to heaven. But do we want to get to heaven and discover how much fun we could have had on the way? Let's choose life now and enjoy life in the way God desires.

2

~⚕~

Watch and Pray

All of you must keep awake (give strict attention, be cautious and active) and watch and pray, that you may not come into temptation. The spirit indeed is willing, but the flesh is weak.

Matthew 26:41

Suppose you knew that your house was surrounded by enemy agents and that at any moment they might break through the door and attack you. Do you think you would be inclined to stay awake and watch the door?

What would you do if for some reason you couldn't stay awake and watch? Wouldn't you make sure someone else in the family was aroused and alerted to the danger?

In this verse, Jesus tells us to keep awake, to give strict attention, to be cautious and active and to watch and pray.

As believers, we are to be constantly alert, alive and watchful. Then, if necessary, we must be ready to take up arms against the attack of the enemy.

Be a Fighter

Fight the good fight of the faith....

1 Timothy 6:12

To be aggressive is to be a fighter.

Just as the apostle Paul said that he had fought the good fight of faith (2 Timothy 4:7), so he instructed his young disciple Timothy to fight the good fight of faith.

In the same way, you and I are to fight the good fight of faith in our daily lives as we struggle against spiritual enemies in high places and in our own mind and heart.

One part of fighting the good fight of faith is being able to recognize the enemy, knowing when things are normal and when things are wrong.

Let me give you an example.

Some time ago I was engaged in a conversation with a certain individual. As I was listening to this person, confusion began to set in. I realized that this happened every time I tried to talk to this person.

Usually I would just go off thinking, "I wonder what's wrong. I don't understand why this happens." I just wasn't comfortable with the person.

The more I thought about it, the more I came to see what the problem was. Every time we would meet and talk I would begin to worry about whether this individual misunderstood something I had done.

The next time we met the same feeling began to rise up in me. But this time I took a more aggressive approach. I just stopped and prayed, "In the name of Jesus Christ, I take authority over this spirit. I am not going to worry. If this person does not like what I did, that is between them and God.

"I have to be free. I can't go all my life making decisions based on what everybody else is going to think. Satan, I will not have this worry. In the name of Jesus, it's over!"

I took a stand, and freedom rushed in. As long as I was passive, Satan tormented me.

That's our problem. We are too passive. Too often we don't move against the enemy when he comes against us with worry or fear or doubt or guilt. We just draw back into a corner somewhere and let him beat us up.

You and I are not supposed to be punching bags for the devil; instead, we are supposed to be fighters.

Now the devil wants us to fight in the natural with everybody around us. But God wants us to forget all the junk that Satan stirs up within us to get us riled up against other people. Instead, He wants us to fight against the spiritual enemies who try to war over our lives and steal our peace and joy.

What Is Normal?

For wherever there is jealousy (envy) and contention (rivalry and selfish ambition), there will also be confusion (unrest, disharmony, rebellion) and all sorts of evil and vile practices.

But the wisdom from above is first of all pure (undefiled); then it is peace-loving, courteous (considerate, gentle). [It is willing to] yield to reason, full of compassion and good fruits; it is wholehearted and straightforward, impartial and unfeigned (free from doubts, wavering, and insincerity).

James 3:16,17

Confusion is not the normal state for a born-again believer, at least not as far as God is concerned. So anytime we feel confusion rising up within us, we need to attack it.

But too often we just go along thinking something is wrong with us rather than realizing the problem is that we are under spiritual attack.

Another mistake we make is trying to figure out everything instead of watching and praying as Jesus commanded us.

Anytime you begin to feel abnormal, anytime you begin to feel oppressed or heavy in spirit, watch and pray. That is how you move into praying without ceasing. (1 Thessalonians 5:17.) You are ready at anytime you sense a need to pray.

But what is normal for the believer? In order to answer that question, let's begin by looking at what is not normal.

It is not normal to worry. It is not normal to be tormented by reasoning, trying to figure out things for which we do not have the answers. It is not normal to be plagued by thoughts of what everybody is going to think of us. It is not normal to be depressed, to feel heavy, to think we are no good. It is not normal to feel we are a failure.

These things may have become normal to some people, but God never intended for these things to be normal. He never intended for life to be that way — for us to live in a state of constant turmoil or torment from our thoughts.

When these kinds of thoughts come upon us, we should be able to recognize them for what they are — lies of the enemy.

In his book, *The Spiritual Man,* under the section entitled, "Weights on the Spirit," Watchman Nee wrote that in those situations: "The spirit needs to be in a state of perfect freedom. It should always be light as though floating in the air.... A Christian ought to realize what the weights laid on his spirit are. Often he feels it is under oppression, as if a thousand pound load were pressing upon his heart.... It is employed by the enemy to harass the spiritual, to deprive him of joy and lightness, as well as to disable his spirit from working together with the Holy Spirit.... A free spirit is the basis for victory.... Whenever the spirit suffers oppression the mind cannot function properly."[1]

All our parts work together. We need to keep ourselves in a state of freedom and a state of normalcy. To do that, we must keep ourselves under the leadership of the Lord Jesus Christ.

The Lordship of Christ

[Inasmuch as we] refute arguments and theories and reasonings and every proud and lofty thing that sets itself up against the [true] knowledge of God; and we lead every thought and purpose away captive into the obedience of Christ (the Messiah, the Anointed One).

2 Corinthians 10:5

The Lord will give us the victory over the devil, but He will do that only as we cry out to Him and ask Him to get involved in our problems.

Nothing is going to change about our situation if all we do is just sit and wish things were different. We have got to take action.

The Lord is ready, willing and able to do something for His people in the area of passivity, apathy, laziness, lethargy and procrastination — all the things which wrap themselves around us and drag us down into depression, discouragement and despair. But we have a part to play also.

We are not a people called to function according to the way we feel. We are a people who are called to take hold of the Word of God and apply it to our lives daily. In order to do that, we must stay spiritually alert — at all times.

3

Six Things To Do Aggressively

And from the days of John the Baptist until the present time, the kingdom of heaven has endured violent assault, and violent men seize it by force [as a precious prize — a share in the heavenly kingdom is sought with most ardent zeal and intense exertion].

Matthew 11:12

We need to take the Kingdom of God — righteousness, peace and joy (Romans 14:17) — by force. As soon as you feel disappointed, aggressively stop the devil at the onset.

From my years of ministry, as well as from my own personal Christian walk, I have learned that there are six things we need to do aggressively.

1. Think aggressively.

> ...what king, going out to engage in conflict with another king, will not first sit down and consider and take counsel whether he is able with ten thousand [men] to meet him who comes against him with twenty thousand?
>
> *Luke 14:31*

A general preparing for battle thinks. He plans and calculates how he can engage and defeat the enemy at the least risk to himself and his army.

You and I need to do the same thing in our Christian warfare as well as in our everyday life.

We need to think, "How can I get out of debt? How can I get my house cleaned up? How can I better provide for my family?"

But we also need to think, "How can I reach more people in my ministry? How can I affect my neighborhood for good? How can I be a blessing to the poor? How can I give more to God?"

Think about it. Ask yourself how you can become more involved and more active in the work of the Lord.

Of course, if you have a family, they must be your first priority and responsibility. You shouldn't get your priorities out of line if you have young children. You need to spend plenty of time with them, especially during their formative years.

But sometimes it is possible to handle both a family and a ministry. I have done it for years. I began my ministry, Life In The Word, when my son was just a year old.

You will find that you can do anything that might at first look impossible, *if* you are called by God to do it and *if* you want to do it badly enough.

Think creatively. Don't just sit around wishing you could do more. Take the initiative and get started.

Think aggressively!

2. *Pray aggressively.*

Let us then fearlessly and confidently and boldly draw near to the throne of grace (the throne of God's unmerited favor to us sinners), that we may receive mercy [for our failures] and find grace to help in good time for every need [appropriate help and well-timed help, coming just when we need it].

Hebrews 4:16

How are we to come before the throne of God? Fearlessly, confidently and boldly.

That means aggressively!

You and I do not have to be bashful or timid with God. We can step forward in confidence and tell Him what we need. We can let Him know that we are expecting Him to do for us what He has promised in His Word.

In Ephesians 3:20 we are told that God is able to "...do superabundantly, far over and above all that we [dare] ask or think [infinitely beyond our highest prayers, desires, thoughts, hopes, or dreams]."

Notice that word "dare." You and I need to be confident, bold, aggressive, daring Christians.

When you approach the throne of God, do so aggressively!

3. Speak aggressively.

> Whoever speaks, [let him do it as one who utters] oracles of God....
>
> *1 Peter 4:11*

As the children of God, you and I are to have an aggressive voice.

Now when I talk about speaking aggressively, I am not talking about being aggressive in the flesh. I am talking about being spiritually aggressive against the forces of evil.

Let me give you an example.

In one place the Bible teaches that we are to be as gentle as doves (Matthew 10:16), but in another place it teaches that we are to be as bold as lions. (Proverbs 28:1.) I used to have a hard time reconciling those two images.

Then I thought about a person who is on the job when his boss who is not a Christian calls him in on the carpet and starts chewing him out unfairly. The worker knows that if he talks back he will get fired, so he just stands there and says nothing, waiting for the Lord to vindicate him.

Although he is gentle as a dove on the outside, on the inside he is as bold as a lion.

In the same way, you and I may sometimes have to stand passively in the flesh, but react aggressively in the spirit. We can allow harsh words to be directed at us physically, but we do not have to receive those words spiritually.

We can refuse to allow ourselves to come under condemnation. We can pray in the Spirit while we are being assaulted in the flesh.

Then once we are out of that situation we can speak forth aggressively from our own mouth, taking authority over the spiritual enemies who are bringing that abuse against us.

Whenever anyone starts coming against me in the flesh, I immediately start praying in the Spirit. I know I don't have to soak up all that abuse, so I protect myself spiritually.

For years I allowed other people to heap all their junk on me. Then later I tried to come against them in the flesh. I finally learned that neither of those tactics works. Since then I have discovered what does work.

I found out the hard way that we war not against flesh and blood but against principalities and powers and spiritual wickedness in high places. So I have learned how to wage spiritual warfare.

You may need to learn to do the same thing. Be as gentle as a dove and as bold as a lion. Develop an aggressive voice.

When you speak to people, don't hang your head and murmur or mumble or whine. Stand up straight, look them in the eye and speak positively, definitively, clearly. Articulate and enunciate. Make yourself understandable.

Don't be mealy-mouthed, insecure, unsure. Be bold enough to open your mouth and say what you have to say with confidence and assurance.

If you are going to sing and worship God then do so aggressively.

Whenever you open your mouth to utter anything, do so as if you are speaking as the oracle of God. Do it enthusiastically, joyfully, graciously — and aggressively.

4. Give aggressively.

Give, and [gifts] will be given to you; good measure, pressed down, shaken together, and running over, will they pour into [the pouch formed by] the bosom [of your robe and used as a bag]. For with the measure you deal out [with the measure you use when you confer benefits on others], it will be measured back to you.

Luke 6:38

When you and I give, we are to give generously and aggressively. Because the way we give is the way we receive.

When we look into our wallet or purse, we are not to pull out the smallest bill we can find. Instead, we are to give as God gives — abundantly.

Now I realize that no offering is too small and none is too great. But at the same time we have got to learn to be as aggressive in our giving as we are in any other aspect of our Christian life.

I seek to be a giver. I desire to give all the time.

One time I was in a Christian bookstore and saw a little offering box for one of those ministries that feeds hungry children. There was a sign beside it that read, "For 50 cents two children can eat for two days."

I started to open my purse and make a donation when a voice inside said to me, "You don't need to do that; you give all the time."

I immediately got violent — spiritually violent! No one could tell on the outside, but I was aroused on the inside. I reached into my purse, pulled out some money and placed it in the box just to prove that I could give as an act of my free will!

You can do the same. Whenever you are tempted to hold back, give more! Show the devil that you are an aggressive giver!

5. *Work aggressively.*

> Whatever your hand finds to do,
> do it with all your might....

> *Ecclesiastes 9:10*

Whatever we put our hand to, we need to do it aggressively.

Don't face any task in your life dreading it and wishing you could escape from it. Stir yourself up in the Holy Spirit and boldly declare, "This is the work that the Lord has given me to do, and with the help of the Holy Spirit I am going to do it with all my might to the glory of God!"

6. Love aggressively.

This is My commandment: that you love one another [just] as I have loved you.

No one has greater love [no one has shown stronger affection] than to lay down (give up) his own life for his friends.

John 15:12,13

As the children of God, we must love others as God loves us. And that means aggressively — and sacrificially.

Love is an effort. We will never love anybody if we are not willing to pay the price.

One time I gave a woman a nice pair of earrings. My flesh wanted to keep them for myself, but my spirit said to be obedient to the Lord and give them away.

Later that woman stood up in a meeting and told how she had been given the earrings she was wearing as "a free gift."

The Lord spoke to me and said, "Yes, it was a free gift to her, but it cost you, just as salvation is a free gift to you but it cost Jesus His life."

Love is the greatest gift of all. When you show forth the love of God, do it freely, sacrificially — and aggressively!

4

⤎

Dealing With Disappointment

According to Webster, to *disappoint* is "to fail to satisfy the hope, desire, or expectation of."[1]

In other words, when we set ourselves to hope, desire or expect something and that hope, desire or expectation is not met, then we become disappointed.

None of us is ever going to get to the place in life that we have no more disappointments. None of us has that much faith. Disappointment is a fact of life, one that must be faced and dealt with because it leads to discouragement, which ultimately leads to devastation if not confronted.

Too often people end up devastated and don't understand why. They don't realize that the problem began a long time ago in simple disappointment, which can be an indication of more serious problems ahead.

Heed the Telltale Signs

If I wake up in the morning sneezing with a slight sore throat and feeling a bit of a headache, I recognize that I am catching a cold. I have found that if I will pray, take some extra vitamin C and A, and get more rest, many times I can head off the sickness.

Disease is often accompanied by early symptoms, signs that something is not right and needs to be attended to before it gets worse.

Disappointment works the same way. It too is preceded by telltale signs that we need to take aggressive action against what we can sense is coming against us.

As we have said, as soon as we detect the first signs that we are under attack by Satan, we must resist him at the onset. It is much more effective to take a stand at the very beginning when we are experiencing disappointment than to wait until we are in the depths of depression and despair.

We all know that it is much easier to forgive someone who has wronged us immediately after the offense than it is to forgive that person after we have given the devil time to work on us and cause us to become angry, bitter and hard.

It is the same with disappointment. It is easier and more effective to deal with it right away than it is to wait until it has evolved into discouragement, depression and devastation.

Causes of Disappointment

Suppose you plan a picnic or barbecue or some other outdoor activity, like a wedding, and it rains.

You have invited all your family and friends, made elaborate preparations and gone to a lot of time and expense to see that everything is just perfect. Then it ends up pouring down, and you are left with a soggy mess.

That is a disappointment. But it is a minor disappointment, one that can be survived.

I have learned that in times like that instead of getting all worked up I have to just say, "Oh, well, that's disappointing, but it's not the end of the world. I'll just have to make the best of it."

Other disappointments are more serious and potentially damaging — especially if they involve people rather than inanimate things, like the weather.

Trust Few

> But Jesus [for His part] did not trust Himself to them, because He knew all [men].

> *John 2:24*

Besides the disappointments we all must bear because life is less than perfect, there are also the disappointments that we have to endure because people themselves are imperfect.

Ultimately, all people, regardless of who they are, will disappoint us if we place too much confidence in them. That is not cynicism or judgmentalism, it is just a fact of life. It is also why it is best not to rely excessively on others — even those who are closest to us.

Now that may sound strange, especially coming from someone who has spent years trying to learn to trust people.

But as we have seen in the life of Jesus, it is possible to trust people to a certain degree without opening up ourselves to them in an unbalanced, unwise manner.

Like Jesus, you and I should love everyone, but we are not required to trust everyone 100 percent. Only a fool does that. Why? Because sooner or later, people will fail us, just as sooner or later we will fail others.

Fallibility is part of being human. And it is the wise person who guards himself against it — in himself and in others.

In many ways, the best solution for disappointment is to avoid it as much as possible. And the best way to do that is to be realistic in our hopes, desires and expectations, especially as they relate to human beings, including ourselves.

> ...A wise son makes a glad father,
> but a foolish...son is the grief of his
> mother.

Proverbs 10:1

Sometimes children are a disappointment to their parents. Today it seems to many mothers and fathers that their children never hear a word they say, that it all goes in one ear and out the other.

I know what that is like. When my son Danny was growing up, he was just like that. I would try to talk to him about something important, and he would just look at me with a blank stare as if he didn't hear a word I was saying.

One time at school he had to stay in during lunch as punishment for something foolish he had done. When I asked why he had done it, he just shrugged his shoulders.

"That's not an answer," I said. "Now tell me, why did you do that?"

"I dunno," he mumbled.

No matter how much I questioned him about why he had done such a foolish thing, his answer was always the same, "I dunno."

So I gave him a little lecture about the importance of behaving himself and paying attention and learning all he could in preparation for his future life.

The very next day I sent him off to school, expecting to see a great improvement in his attitude and behavior. Instead, he came home with a note from the teacher saying that Danny had had the worst day since school started.

That kind of thing is disappointing to a parent. And often it gets worse the older the child gets, because more is expected of him.

The greater the hope, desire and expectation, the greater the disappointment. But even minor incidents can cause frustration and bitter disappointment that can lead to more serious problems if not dealt with promptly and properly.

The Little Foxes That Spoil the Vines

> Take us the foxes, the little foxes,
> that spoil the vines....

Song of Solomon 2:15 KJV

Little disappointments can create frustration, which in turn may lead to bigger problems that can produce a great deal of damage.

Besides the huge disappointments that occur when we fail to get the job or promotion or house we wanted, we can become just as upset and frustrated by a series of minor annoyances.

For example, suppose someone is supposed to meet you for lunch and fails to show up. Or suppose you make a special trip downtown or to the mall to buy a certain sale item at a discount, then when you get there it is all sold out. Or suppose you get all dressed up for a special occasion and suddenly notice at the last minute that there is an unsightly rip in your clothes.

All these kinds of things are actually minor, but they can add up to cause a lot of grief. That's why we have got to know how to handle them and keep them in perspective. Otherwise, they can get out of hand and be blown up all out of proportion. That, in turn, can open us up to serious problems when we are faced with a real challenge.

Let me give you an example.

Imagine you start out your day behind time, so you are already frustrated. On the way to the office, the traffic causes you to be even later than you intended.

Then when you do finally get to work you find out that someone on the job has been gossiping about you behind your back.

You go get some coffee to help you calm down and get a hold on yourself, and you spill it all over yourself — and you have an important meeting with the boss and no time to change!

All of those things pile up one on the other until you are in a real stew.

Then just about that time you get a report from the doctor that is not in line with your hope and prayers, and to top it all off your fiancé calls and threatens to break your engagement that has been announced to the whole world!

What is likely to be your reaction — faith or fury?

All those minor frustrations with the traffic and gossip and the coffee have set you up for a major calamity when you have to face some really serious problem like sickness or a failed relationship.

That's why we have to be on our guard against the little foxes that destroy the vines, because all together they can do just as much damage as the serious disappointments that often accompany or follow them.

We must learn to do as Paul did in the book of Acts when the serpent attached itself to his hand — he simply shook it off! (Acts 28:1-5.) If we practice dealing quickly with disappointments as they come, they will not pile up into a mountain of devastation.

5

⤬

Confidence in Jesus

Why are you cast down, O my
inner self? And why should you
moan over me and be disquieted
within me? Hope in God and wait
expectantly for Him, for I shall yet
praise Him, my Help and my God.

Psalm 42:5

You and I must have our hope in God
because we never know what is going to
come against us in this life.

In several places in the Bible, for example
in 1 Corinthians 10:4, Jesus is referred to as
the Rock. The apostle Paul goes on to tell us
in Colossians 2:7 that we are to be rooted
and grounded in Him.

Nowhere are we taught to be rooted and grounded in other people or in our job or in our church or in our friends or even in ourselves.

If we get our roots wrapped around the Rock of Jesus Christ, we are in good shape. But if we get them wrapped around anything or anyone else, we are in trouble.

Nothing nor no one is going to be as solid and dependable and immovable as Jesus. That's why I don't want people to get rooted and grounded in me or my ministry. I want to point people to Jesus. I know that ultimately I will fail them in some way, just as I know they will ultimately fail me.

That's the problem with us humans; we are always liable to failure.

But Jesus Christ isn't.

Be rooted and grounded in Jesus. Put your hope wholly and unchangeably in Him. Not in man, not in circumstances, not in your bank account, not in your job, not in anything or anyone else.

If you don't put your hope and faith in the Rock of your salvation, you are headed for disappointment, which leads to discouragement and devastation.

People Are Faulty

Confidence in an unfaithful man
in time of trouble is like a broken
tooth or a foot out of joint.

Proverbs 25:19

Some time ago my daughter was engaged to be married. The ring had been picked out, the money saved and the wedding plans made.

Then a short time after the engagement was announced, the whole thing was called off because of the infidelity and dishonesty of the groom.

It was really a sad situation, especially for the lovely, wonderful, sweet, young bride-to-be who had suffered many other hard disappointments in her short life.

But this time she got the jump on the devil. Rather than getting upset and feeling sorry for herself, she said, "Well, thank God I found out what kind of a man he really is now before the wedding and not somewhere down the road when it would have been too late to do anything about it."

I was so proud of her and so pleased with the way she handled that terribly disappointing situation.

Although she knew it was best that it happen before the wedding rather than afterward, she was still hurt. So her father and I encouraged her, counseled her and prayed with her.

In addition, she began to listen to some of my teaching tapes and read books that encourage and uplift the spirit.

She came through that difficult, trying time because her faith and trust were not in faulty man but in the never-failing Jesus. She kept looking to Him as her example of perseverance in the face of disappointment and discouragement. That is what each one of us needs to learn to do.

Today she is married to a wonderful man, and she and her husband both work in the ministry with us.

Keep On Looking to Jesus

...let us run with patient endurance and steady and active persistence the appointed course of the race that is set before us.

Looking away [from all that will detract] to Jesus, Who is the Leader and the Source of our faith [giving the first incentive for our belief] and is also its Finisher [bringing it to maturity and perfection]. He, for the joy [of obtaining the prize] that was set before Him, endured the cross, despising and ignoring the shame,

and is now seated at the right hand
of the throne of God.

Just think of Him Who endured
from sinners such grievous opposi-
tion and bitter hostility against
Himself [reckon up and consider it
all in comparison with your trials],
so that you may not grow weary or
exhausted, losing heart and relaxing
and fainting in your minds.

Hebrews 12:1-3

It does not take any special talent to give
up, to lie down on the side of the road of life
and say, "I quit." Any unbeliever can do that.

You don't have to be a Christian to be a
quitter.

But once you get hold of Jesus, or better
yet when He gets hold of you, He begins to
pump strength and energy and courage into
you, and something strange and wonderful
begins to happen. He won't let you quit!

You may say, "Oh, Lord, just leave me alone. I don't want to go on anymore." But He won't let you give up, even if you want to.

I used to want to give up and quit. But now I get out of bed and start each day afresh and anew. I begin my day by praying and reading the Bible and speaking the Word, seeking after God.

The devil may be screaming in my ear, "That's not doing you one bit of good. You've been doing that for years, and look what it's got you, you still have trouble."

That's when I say, "Shut up, devil! The Bible says that I am to look to Jesus and follow His example. He is my Leader, the Source and Finisher of my faith."

That is what my daughter did to keep up her spirits and to keep going in spite of what had happened to her. She could have looked at her past record and said, "Well, it has happened to me again — more rejection. It happened once, then twice, and now it has happened the third time." Instead, she kept looking to Jesus.

You and I need to make a decision today that, come what may, we are going to keep pressing on no matter what.

Get Reappointed

> Live in harmony with one another; do not be haughty (snobbish, high-minded, exclusive), but readily adjust yourself to [people, things] and give yourselves to humble tasks. Never overestimate yourself or be wise in your own conceits.
>
> *Romans 12:16*

Recently I have been thinking about what all the Lord has done for me in the course of my life and ministry. It is amazing now that I look back on it. But it was not always easy. There were many times when I wanted desperately to give up and quit.

I have shared with you how, when I would get down and discouraged, the Lord would say to me, "Joyce, when disappointment comes, you have got to get reappointed, because if you don't you will end up in discouragement and that will lead to devastation."

That's why we must learn to adapt and adjust, to change direction. That's what my daughter did, and it has led her into a totally new and different life.

Now, of course, it won't always be easy. It is a lot harder to adjust to a broken engagement than it is to adjust to a rained-out picnic. But the answer is still the same regardless of the circumstances that must be faced and dealt with.

Unless we learn to get reappointed, to adapt and adjust, to get a new direction, we will never discover or enjoy the wonderful new and exciting life that God has in store for us.

6

⊱

Meditate on the Things of God

Do not fret or have any anxiety about anything, but in every circumstance and in everything, by prayer and petition (definite requests), with thanksgiving, continue to make your wants known to God.

And God's peace [shall be yours, that tranquil state of a soul assured of its salvation through Christ, and so fearing nothing from God and being content with its earthly lot of whatever sort that is, that peace] which transcends all understanding shall garrison and mount guard over your hearts and minds in Christ Jesus.

Philippians 4:6,7

If you don't want to be devastated by discouragement, then don't meditate on your disappointments.

Did you know that your feelings are hooked up to your thinking? If you don't think that is true, just take about twenty minutes or so and think about nothing but your problems. I can assure you that by the end of that time your feelings and maybe even your countenance will have changed. You may have become depressed or angry or upset. Yet your situation will not have changed a bit.

That's why you can go to church and sing songs, hear sermons, then go away with the same negative attitude and outlook you had when you left home. It is because you sat there in church and meditated on your problems rather than focusing your mind and spirit on the Lord.

With Whom Do You Fellowship?

In one issue of my monthly magazine, I asked this question: "Do you fellowship with God or with your problem?"

The reason I asked that question of my readers is because that is what the Lord asked me one morning.

I got up that day with my mind thinking about my problem. Suddenly the Spirit of the Lord spoke to me. I could tell by the tone of His voice He was a little bit aggravated with me.

He said to me, "Joyce, are you going to fellowship with your problem or with Me?" Then He went on to say to me what I am saying to you, "Don't meditate on your disappointments."

When you get disappointed, don't sit around and feel sorry for yourself, because despite how you may feel you are no different from anyone else.

Sometimes that is a bit hard for us to realize because the devil tries hard to make us think we are the only one who has ever had a bad deal.

That's not true.

One time I encouraged my daughter greatly because I sat down with her and shared with her what my life was like from age eighteen through twenty-three. By the time I was done, she felt really blessed in her own life.

Like everyone else, she has had some unfortunate things happen to her from time to time, but for years and years my life was one long horrible disaster.

For example, I told her about the time I was eighteen or nineteen years old and found myself sitting in a rooming house in Oakland, California, three thousand miles from home, with no car, no television, no telephone and no one to care about me. I told her how I would sit there every night and write sad poems and feel sorry for myself, and then get up the next morning and walk to work.

"Thank God you have a good family, a good job, a good home and a good car," I told her, "because I had none of those things."

By the time I had finished telling her my life story, she was excited abut her present situation and her future prospects.

That's the choice each of us has. We can get excited by thinking about what all we have or can have, or we can get discouraged by thinking about what all we don't have.

The fact is, if we don't have it, we don't have it, and sitting around wishing we did is not going to change anything. We might wish it did, but it doesn't.

If we want to overcome disappointment and avoid the discouragement and devastation it leads to, we have got to be realistic and deal with the facts.

And the fact is, as bad as things may seem, we still have a choice. We can choose to fellowship with our problems or fellowship with God.

No matter what we have lost or how bad we may feel, we still have the ability to direct our thoughts away from the negative and toward the positive.

Think On These Things!

For the rest, brethren, whatever is true, whatever is worthy of reverence and is honorable and seemly, whatever is just, whatever is pure, whatever is lovely and lovable, whatever is kind and winsome and gracious, if there is any virtue and excellence, if there is anything worthy of praise, think on and weigh and take account of these things [fix your minds on them].

Philippians 4:8

In verses 6 and 7 of this passage we are told that if we have a problem we are not to worry or fret but to take it to God in prayer. We are assured that if we will do that, the peace of the Lord will keep us from fear and anxiety and will mount a guard over our mind and heart.

But here in verse 8 we see that there is something else we must do in order to receive and enjoy the marvelous joy and peace of the Lord. We must take control of our thought life. We have to direct our mind away from the negative toward the positive.

Now you may notice that the first thing we are told to do is to think on whatever is true. That does not mean we are to think on the bad things that have happened to us in the past because they did actually happen.

There is a difference between truth and fact. Things that happened in the past are fact, but Jesus and the Word are Truth, and they are greater than fact.

Let me explain by using an example from the life of a friend of ours.

Some time ago this friend's husband died and went to be with the Lord. He is now in heaven, and she will not see him again until she gets there.

That is fact.

But the truth is not that her life is over and now she has nothing to live for. The devil would like for her to believe that, but it is not so.

The fact is that the young man to whom my daughter was engaged lied to her and hurt her deeply. But the truth is that her life did not end with that disappointment. The truth is that she still had her whole life ahead of her, and it was filled with many blessings.

The fact is that she had lost a fiancé, but the truth is that she still had a future, a fine Christian home and family, her own car, a good job, caring friends and the love of God.

This loss occurred just before her nineteenth birthday. That was quite a birthday present, wasn't it? But instead of becoming sad and bitter, she chose to take a different perspective and approach.

She said, "Tomorrow is my nineteenth birthday, and as far as I am concerned it is the first day of the rest of my life!"

I was so impressed by her attitude and outlook that I bought her a small diary and told her, "Write in this little book all the miracles that God does for you this coming year. On your twentieth birthday, we will read them and celebrate together."

And that is just what we did.

That is what you and I must do too. Although we do not always have the power to keep disappointments from happening to us, we do have the power to choose how we are going to react to them.

We can allow our thoughts to dwell on them until we become totally discouraged and devastated, or we can focus our attention on all the good things that have happened to us in our life — and on all the good things that God still has in store for us in the days ahead.

7

⤳

Hope and Expectation

[For my determined purpose is] that I may know Him [that I may progressively become more deeply and intimately acquainted with Him, perceiving and recognizing and understanding the wonders of His Person more strongly and more clearly], and that I may in the same way come to know the power outflowing from His resurrection [which it exerts over believers], and that I may so share His sufferings as to be continually transformed [in spirit into His likeness even] to His death....

Philippians 3:10

In this verse Paul said he had done something which I think we all need to do: He had
set a goal for himself.

You and I have got to have a goal. We
have got to have hope and direction and
expectation in life.

Sometimes when people have been disappointed over and over and over, they lose
their direction and expectation. They become afraid to put their hope in anything or
anyone for fear they will be disappointed
again. They hate the pain of disappointment
so much they would rather never believe at
all than to run the risk of being hurt.

The sad part is that in the game of life
they are the losers not the winners because
victory comes only with risk.

Hurt Breeds Suspicion

That if possible I may attain to the
[spiritual and moral] resurrection

[that lifts me] out from among the
dead [even while in the body].

Philippians 3:11

When a girl has been hurt two or three
times by a boy she cares about, she thinks,
"I'll never trust anyone again."

That is exactly what the devil wants all of
us to do.

If you and I have friends who fail us or let
us down, Satan wants us to say, "That's it;
I'll never trust anyone again."

When we do that, we are playing right
into the devil's hands.

Someone once said, "If you get hurt, you
get suspicious."

That may be true, but it is just another one
of the devices the enemy uses to deceive us
and keep us from reaching our God-given
goal in life.

Satan wants us to believe that everybody
is like the ones who have disappointed us.

But they aren't.

The devil always tries to take a few bad experiences and use them to convince us we should never trust anyone in life.

If you have been hurt, don't start thinking you can't trust anybody. If you do, you will allow Satan to rob you of many of God's greatest blessings.

The apostle Paul had a goal, a spiritual dream. He wanted to get to the place that no matter what happened to him in life, it did not affect him or keep him from living this earthly life to the fullest while fulfilling his God-given purpose.

In order to reach that goal, he had to take risks. He not only had to trust God, he also had to trust other people. He had to open himself up to the risk of harm and loss.

So do you and I. We have got to keep going despite everything the enemy may throw in our path to cause us to become discouraged, give up and quit short of attaining our ideal.

Press On!

Not that I have now attained [this ideal], or have already been made perfect, but I press on to lay hold of (grasp) and make my own, that for which Christ Jesus (the Messiah) has laid hold of me and made me His own.

I do not consider, brethren, that I have captured and made it my own [yet]; but one thing I do [it is my one aspiration]; forgetting what lies behind and straining forward to what lies ahead,

I press on toward the goal to win the [supreme and heavenly] prize to which God in Christ Jesus is calling us upward.

Philippians 3:12-14

In verse 12 Paul says that although he has not yet reached his goal or attained his ideal, he is not quitting. Instead, he is pressing on.

Then in verse 13 he goes on to say that there is one thing he does.

This one thing should be of interest and importance to us because it comes from the man who wrote two-thirds of the New Testament by revelation of the Holy Spirit.

What was that one principle by which the great apostle Paul operated in his life that he believed was responsible for bringing him into the fulfillment of his dreams and goals?

There are two parts to this principle: The first is forgetting that which lies behind in the past, and the second is pressing on toward that which lies ahead in the future.

That is an important lesson for all of us to learn.

For example, consider the woman who lost her husband. When we say that she should forget that which lies behind in the past and press on toward what lies ahead in the future, we are not suggesting that she should forget all about her husband and never remember him. We are just saying that if she focuses her mind too much on her old life, it will get her into trouble. She will be living in the past rather than pressing on toward the future.

I am reminded of a woman in our church whose son died of leukemia at the age of sixteen. We had all prayed and believed God for him to be healed, but it did not happen; he still went to be with the Lord. Yet in the midst of that tragic loss the Lord sustained this young mother.

One day after the memorial service, she was doing the laundry and came across one of her son's shirts. As she picked it up and hugged it, she began to weep uncontrollably. She said later that she could feel the grief taking hold of her.

Realizing what was happening to her, she suddenly began speaking the name of Jesus. Grabbing up one of her son's shirts, she boldly declared, "Satan, see this. I am going to use it as a garment of praise. I am not going to sink into grief, but I am going to rise up in praise!"

It is natural to grieve over what has happened in the past, but only to a point and only for a certain time. Sooner or later we must come to grips with our grief and loss and decide to put it behind us and get on with our life.

Paul is talking about our imperfections when he speaks of forgetting what lies behind and pressing on toward what lies ahead, but we can apply the principle to all of life.

If we are to accomplish what God has called us and anointed us and commissioned us to achieve in this life, then like Paul we must have a goal and keep pressing toward it.

8

❧

A New Thing

Do not [earnestly] remember the former things; neither consider the things of old.

Behold, I am doing a new thing! Now it springs forth; do you not perceive and know it and will you not give heed to it?....

Isaiah 43:18,19

In dealing with the past, the danger we must avoid is allowing it to keep us in grief for what has been rather than in gratitude for what is and in anticipation of what is yet to be.

To launch my own ministry I had to leave a position as associate pastor at a church. It was a very hard thing to do, and for a long time I grieved over the loss of relationships with the people in that church and the things we used to do together that I was no longer a part of.

I had to let go of the past to go on, but my mind and emotions were trying to hang onto it. Finally I won the victory. I became excited about the future, but at the same time I was still disappointed about losing the position and the close relationships with the people.

The disappointment was adversely affecting the joy of my new ministry. It was a confusing time for me, but through it I learned a lot about letting go of what lies behind and pressing on to what lies ahead.

Over and over God has to remind me, "You have to let go of what lies behind. The past is not your life anymore. Now I am doing a new thing."

I AM!

And God said to Moses...You shall say this to the Israelites: I AM has sent me to you!

God said also to Moses, This shall you say to the Israelites: The Lord, the God of your fathers, of Abraham, of Isaac, and of Jacob, has sent me to you! This is My name forever, and by this name I am to be remembered to all generations.

Exodus 3:14,15

If you and I concentrate too long on the past, it will get us into trouble. That's why from time to time the Lord has to remind us, as He did Moses and the Israelites, that He is the I AM, not the I WAS.

We need to remember all the good things that God has done for us in the past, just as He did for Abraham and Isaac and Jacob and all the other faithful men and women of the Bible. But we must not become so attuned to past joys and victories that we fail to appreciate and enjoy what God is doing for us now — and what He has in store for us in the future.

In John 8:58 we read, "Jesus replied, I assure you, most solemnly I tell you, before Abraham was born, I AM." Hebrews 13:8 tells us that "Jesus Christ (the Messiah) is [always] the same, yesterday, today, [yes] and forever (to the ages)."

That is the way our faith is to be — always, eternal, timeless, unchanging — now!

Don't Look Back!

> Jesus said to him, No one who puts his hand to the plow and looks back [to the things behind] is fit for the kingdom of God.
>
> *Luke 9:62*

God does not want us living in the past. He knows that even if we could go back and recreate everything just as it was in days gone by, it would still not be the same. Do you know why? Because that was then, and this is now.

Yesterday is gone; it is lost in the recesses of time. This is now. We have got a now God, we are a now people, and we must live a now life — one day at a time.

So often people lose their joy because they had something in the past that made them joyful but which is now gone. Many are pining away for the move of God that was, but is not any more.

It is too bad it no longer exists, but it doesn't, and there is nothing you or I can do about it. Instead, we must learn to live in the present. God is moving now — let's enjoy now!

We must put the past behind us and get on with what God is doing in our life where we are at the moment.

Thank God we can press on to what He has in store for us, but in the meantime we need to keep our hand to the plow and quit looking back to what once was and will never be again.

Turn Back or Press On?

Now those people who talk as they did show plainly that they are in search of a fatherland (their own country).

If they had been thinking with [homesick] remembrance of that country from which they were emigrants, they would have found constant opportunity to return to it.

But the truth is that they were yearning for and aspiring to a better and more desirable country, that is, a heavenly [one]. For that reason God is not ashamed to be called their God [even to be surnamed their God — the God of Abraham, Isaac, and Jacob], for He has prepared a city for them.

Hebrews 11:14-16

This passage is referring to the Israelites who were led out of their previous home but who had to go through some difficult, trying times to get to their new home.

It says that if they had been thinking with homesick remembrance of that country they had just left, they would have had ample opportunity to return to it. Instead, they were looking for a new homeland, one prepared for them by God, and so they kept pressing on despite obstacles and hardships.

That is the choice you and I must make. We can choose to look back with homesick remembrance, or we can choose to look ahead with joyful anticipation.

This passage does not mean to suggest that we are never to recall the good times from our past or never bring to mind our departed loved ones. It just means that we are not to keep our mind and heart constantly turned toward the past, because if we do we will miss what God has for us in the future.

That's why we need to make a vow that we are not going to waste our lives in looking back, but we are going to press on to what lies ahead.

This is a *today* message. It is something we can and must do today and every new day we live.

I used to think this word about forgetting the past applied only to previous mistakes and failures. Then one day I realized I was making myself just as miserable by constantly reliving my past victories and successes.

When a thing is finished, we should let the curtain fall on it and go on to the next thing without making comparisons between them. We should not compare present mistakes or victories with past mistakes or victories. If we do, we will open ourselves up to either discouragement or pride.

We should completely enjoy our life as we are presently experiencing it. We can do that by not comparing it to experiences or segments of our life in the past.

That's why the Lord has told us in Isaiah 43:18,19 not to remember the former things, nor even consider the things of old. Why? Because they are gone, and now God is doing a new thing. It is springing up right before our eyes, and we need to perceive it and give heed to it if we want to be a part of it and benefit from it.

Sow in Tears, Reap in Joy

> They who sow in tears shall reap
> in joy and singing.
>
> *Psalm 126:5*

No matter what has happened to us in the past, or is happening to us now, our life is not over. And we must not let the devil convince us it is.

Our enemy will try to tell us that we made one mistake too many, and now it's too late for us.

We must not listen to him. Instead, we must tell him, "Satan, you are a liar and the father of all lies. This is a new day, and I am expecting a miracle."

The reason we go through life expecting a miracle at anytime is because we never know when it is going to come. We never know when God is going to pass our way. That's what makes life so exciting.

The devil would like for us to think our time will never come and our miracle will never happen. But if we keep ourselves rooted and grounded in Jesus Christ, eventually our time *will* come, and our miracle *will* happen.

But we have to be prepared for it. To do that we must keep Satan from discouraging us so much that we quit and give up. If we do, then no matter what God has planned for us, it won't happen.

That's why God keeps urging us throughout the Bible not to become dismayed or discouraged or give up, because He knows that although "...weeping may endure for a night,...joy comes in the morning" (Psalm 30:5).

God Will Finish His Work

And I am convinced and sure of this very thing, that He Who began a good work in you will continue until the day of Jesus Christ [right up to the time of His return], developing [that good work] and perfecting and bringing it to full completion in you.

Philippians 1:6

God never starts anything He does not intend to finish. He is the Author and the Finisher. (Hebrews 12:2.)

Too often the problem is not God, it is us. We are stuck in the past, in the old thing, so we fail to perceive and heed the new thing God is doing in the here and now. The reason we can't give heed to the new thing is because we are still hanging on to the old thing, as good as it may have been.

What God did for us yesterday is wonderful, but He has the capacity to do twice as much for us today and tomorrow.

The question we must ask ourselves is: Which do we want? The old thing or the new thing?

9

⤫

New Wine, New Wineskins

He told them a proverb also: No one puts a patch from a new garment on an old garment; if he does, he will both tear the new one, and the patch from the new [one] will not match the old [garment].

And no one pours new wine into old wineskins; if he does, the fresh wine will burst the skins and it will be spilled and the skins will be ruined (destroyed).

But new wine must be put into fresh wineskins.

Luke 5:36-38

In recent years the Lord has given me a whole new understanding of this passage.

I used to think it applied only to salvation by grace rather than salvation by keeping the law. Now I see it applies to the new lifestyle and mindset of those who have been made new creatures in Christ Jesus.

You and I are always wanting to get the new but hold on to the old. But Jesus says that is not possible. To illustrate His point, He tells a proverb about not sewing a new patch into an old garment or putting new wine in old wineskins.

The Sewing Proverb

Anyone who knows anything about sewing knows that you cannot put a new patch on an old garment.

If you have an old garment that has been washed and shrunk and faded, and you try to patch a hole in it by using a piece of new material, through time the new cloth will shrink and tear. Even if it doesn't, the new piece will not match the old garment because it has not yet become worn and faded by time and washing.

In this part of the proverb, Jesus is telling us not to try to take our new life and patch it into the old life. It just won't work.

Neither will it work to try to put new wine into old wineskins.

Which Is Better?

> And no one after drinking old wine
> immediately desires new wine, for
> he says, The old is good or better.

Luke 5:39

Do you know why a person says the old wine is better than the new wine? He says it for the same reason you and I prefer the old life to the new. Because the old is more comfortable.

Most of us prefer the old life to the new life because we are used to it. Even though there is a part of us that wants the new wine, the new thing, the new day, the new move, there is another part of us that wants to hang onto the old because it is what we are most comfortable with.

Rather than moving on with the Lord, we try to stay where we are because it is so much easier.

Moving on is hard.

It is hard to move to a new town, make new friends, find a new doctor and school and church. (Sometimes it is even hard for me to put a piece of furniture someplace new!) It is so much more appealing just to stay where we are and enjoy what we have and know.

But what we tend to forget is that as Christians we ourselves have been made new.

The New Has Come!

> Therefore if any person is [ingrafted] in Christ (the Messiah) he is a new creation (a new creature altogether); the old [previous moral and spiritual condition] has passed away, Behold, the fresh and new has come!
>
> *2 Corinthians 5:17*

You and I must realize and understand that we are new creatures in Christ Jesus. We have been called to a whole new life in Him. We must not be so afraid to let go of what we were and had in our old life that we cannot freely receive and enjoy what God has for us in our new life.

I came to see this when the Lord spoke to me and said, "Don't you realize, Joyce, that this is the foundation for the new creation reality: that old things are passed away and all things have become brand new?"

That is not true just when we answer an altar call and make a decision for Christ. It is an ongoing principle of the new creation lifestyle.

Out With the Old, In With the New!

Because God had us in mind and had something better and greater in view for us....

Hebrews 11:40

Have you realized yet that what you now have would not be so bad if you would simply quit comparing it with what you used to have?

When we go to minister in India, where the poverty and living conditions are absolutely horrible, the condition of the people there disturbs us more than it does them. Why? They have nothing else to compare to the way they live.

What the people in India we see have today is what they have always had. We, of course, have always lived in America, a land of abundance. Therefore, when we go to India, everywhere we look we see conditions that are almost unspeakably horrible *compared* to the conditions we have always known.

What's the sense of living day by day discouraged and depressed and downtrodden because of your old life that no longer exists?

Don't sit around and consider the old things. Don't remember the former things anymore. That is all gone now, replaced by something new and better, if you only knew it.

Press on to those things that lie ahead.

What are you to do when disappointment comes — which it will because it is a fact of life? It may be a little thing or a huge thing. It may be as insignificant as a rained-out picnic or as significant as a broken engagement.

Whatever form it may take, disappointment is going to come. When it does weigh upon you like a rock, you can either let it press you down so that you become discouraged and even devastated, or you can use it as a steppingstone to higher and better things.

There is no way you can sit around and think negatively and have a positive life. It won't work. The more you think about your disappointments, the more discouraged you are going to get. And if you are discouraged long enough, you will become devastated. And when you get devastated, you are in big trouble.

But God has better things for you than that!

This is a new day. So the next time disappointment comes your way, get reappointed. Adapt and adjust. Forget what lies behind and press on to what lies ahead.

Remember that the Lord is doing a new thing in your life. So forget the past and live in the fullness and joy of the new life He has planned and prepared for you.

Conclusion

⤫

May Christ through your faith [actually] dwell (settle down, abide, make His permanent home) in your hearts! May you be rooted deep in love and founded securely on love.

Ephesians 3:17

I encourage you to be careful about where you place your hope and confidence.

In Ephesians 3:17 we are told to be rooted and grounded in love. We are to be rooted and grounded in the love of Christ Jesus — in Him — not other people, our children, our friends, our job, etc.

Jesus is called the Rock. He is a rock that is never going to move.

If you get your roots wrapped around the Rock, when minor disappointments come along you will be able to say, "Oh, well," and get on with your life. When major disappointments come, you can receive emotional healing from the Lord and through His power you can decide to go on.

If you are rooted and grounded in anything else, you will end up disappointed, discouraged, depressed and devastated, because nothing else and no one else is rock solid — only Jesus!

Learn to adapt and adjust. You can do it! Why should you do it? For your own sake.

Count it a privilege to adapt and adjust to different people and situations.

Don't meditate on the disappointment that comes into your life. Let it go and let God take care of you. Face the disappointment at its onset and be quick to make any adjustments required to remedy the situation.

Instead of concentrating on your problems and getting discouraged, focus on God. Meditate on His promises. Confess His Word and submit yourself and your situation to Him in prayer.

Take an inventory of what you have left, not just what you have lost. This keeps your mind in the present where God is. Remember, Jesus called Himself, "I AM," not "I WAS" or "I WILL BE." He is here for you right now. Today you can begin enjoying life!

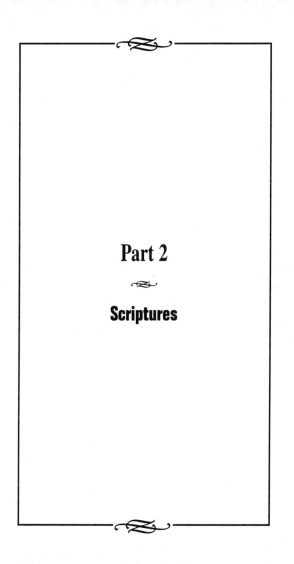

Part 2

Scriptures

Scriptures
To Combat Discouragement

[What, what would have become of me] had I not believed that I would see the Lord's goodness in the land of the living!

Wait and hope for and expect the Lord; be brave and of good courage and let your heart be stout and enduring. Yes, wait for and hope for and expect the Lord.

Psalm 27:13,14

I have seen that everything [human] has its limits and end [no matter how extensive, noble, and excellent]; but Your commandment is exceedingly broad and extends without limits [into eternity].

Psalm 119:96

Confidence in an unfaithful man in time of trouble is like a broken tooth or a foot out of joint.

Proverbs 25:19

For I know the thoughts and plans that I have for you, says the Lord, thoughts and plans for welfare and peace and not for evil, to give you hope in your final outcome.

Jeremiah 29:11

But as for me, I will look to the Lord and confident in Him I will keep watch; I will wait with hope and expectancy for the God of my salvation; my God will hear me.

Micah 7:7

Live in harmony with one another; do not be haughty (snobbish, high-minded, exclusive), but readily adjust yourself to [people, things] and give yourselves to humble tasks.

Never overestimate yourself or be wise in your own conceits.

Romans 12:16

Beloved, never avenge yourselves, but leave the way open for [God's] wrath; for it is written, Vengeance is Mine, I will repay (requite), says the Lord.

Romans 12:19

God is faithful (reliable, trustworthy, and therefore ever true to His promise, and He can be depended on); by Him you were called into companionship and participation with His Son, Jesus Christ our Lord.

1 Corinthians 1:9

...What eye has not seen and ear has not heard and has not entered into the heart of man, [all that] God has prepared (made and keeps ready) for those who love Him [who hold Him in affectionate reverence, promptly obeying Him and gratefully recognizing the benefits He has bestowed].

1 Corinthians 2:9

But thanks be to God, Who in Christ always leads us in triumph [as trophies of Christ's victory] and through us spreads and makes evident the fragrance of the knowledge of God everywhere.

2 Corinthians 2:14

And let us not lose heart and grow weary and faint in acting nobly and doing right, for in due time and at the appointed season we shall reap, if we do not loosen and relax our courage and faint.

Galatians 6:9

For He foreordained us (destined us, planned in love for us) to be adopted (revealed) as His own children through Jesus Christ, in accordance with the purpose of His will [because it pleased Him and was His kind intent] —

[So that we might be] to the praise and the commendation of His glorious grace (favor and mercy), which He so freely bestowed on us in the Beloved.

Ephesians 1:5,6

Now to Him Who, by (in consequence of) the [action of His] power that is at work within us, is able to [carry out His purpose and] do superabundantly, far over and above all that we [dare] ask or think [infinitely beyond our highest prayers, desires, thoughts, hopes, or dreams].

Ephesians 3:20

And as for you, brethren, do not become weary or lose heart in doing

right [but continue in well-doing
without weakening].

2 Thessalonians 3:13

Prayer for Overcoming Discouragement

Father, Your Word is a lamp to my feet and a light to my path.

Keep me, I pray, from hanging my hopes and expectations on people like me, because we are all very capable of disappointing one another.

Let me release forgiveness toward those who have failed me in the past and to let go of the painful memories of those disappointments.

Increase in me, Lord, that I may be more and more like You, and less and less like me.

These things I ask in Jesus' holy name, amen.

Prayer for a Personal Relationship With the Lord

~≥~

If you have never invited Jesus, the Prince of Peace, to be your Lord and Savior, I invite you to do so now. Pray the following prayer, and if you are really sincere about it, you will experience a new life in Christ.

Father,

You loved the world so much, You gave Your only begotten Son to die for our sins so that whoever believes in Him will not perish, but have eternal life.

Your Word says we are saved by grace through faith as a gift from You. There is nothing we can do to earn salvation.

I believe and confess with my mouth that Jesus Christ is Your Son, the Savior of the world. I believe He died on the cross for me and bore all of my sins, paying the price for them. I believe in my heart that You raised Jesus from the dead.

I ask You to forgive my sins. I confess Jesus as my Lord. According to Your Word, I am saved and will spend eternity with You! Thank You, Father. I am so grateful! In Jesus' name, amen.

See John 3:16; Ephesians 2:8,9; Romans 10:9,10; 1 Corinthians 15:3,4; 1 John 1:9; 4:14-16; 5:1,12,13.

Endnotes

✒

Chapter 1

[1] *Webster's II New College Dictionary* (Boston/New York: Houghton Mifflin Company, 1995), s.v. "oppress."

[2] *Webster's II,* s.v. "aggressive," "enterprising."

Chapter 2

[1] Watchman Nee, *The Spiritual Man,* Vol. 1 (New York: Christian Fellowship Publishers, Inc, 1968), p. 145.

Chapter 4

[1] *Webster's II,* s.v. "disappoint."

About the Author

Joyce Meyer has been teaching the Word of God since 1976 and in full-time ministry since 1980. As an associate pastor at Life Christian Center in St. Louis, Missouri, she developed, coordinated and taught a weekly meeting known as "Life In The Word." After more than five years, the Lord brought it to a conclusion, directing her to establish her own ministry and call it "Life In The Word, Inc."

Joyce's "Life In The Word" radio broadcast is heard on over 250 stations nationwide. Joyce's 30-minute "Life In The Word With Joyce Meyer" television program was released in 1993 and is broadcast throughout the United States and several foreign countries. Her teaching tapes are enjoyed internationally. She travels extensively conducting Life In The Word conferences, as well as speaking in local churches.

Joyce and her husband, Dave, business administrator at Life In The Word, have been married for 31 years and are the parents of four children. Three are married, and their youngest son resides with them in Fenton, Missouri, a St. Louis suburb.

Joyce believes the call on her life is to establish believers in God's Word. She says, "Jesus died to set the captives free, and far too many Christians have little or no victory in their daily lives." Finding herself in the same situation many years ago, and having found freedom to live in victory through applying God's Word, Joyce goes equipped to set captives free and to exchange *ashes for beauty*.

Joyce has taught on emotional healing and related subjects in meetings all over the country, helping multiplied thousands. She has recorded over 170 different audio cassette albums and is the author of 27 books to help the Body of Christ on various topics.

Her "Emotional Healing Package" contains over 23 hours of teaching on the subject. Albums included in this package are: "Confidence"; "Beauty for Ashes" (includes a syllabus); "Managing Your Emotions"; "Bitterness, Resentment, and Unforgiveness"; "Root of Rejection"; and a 90-minute Scripture/music tape entitled, "Healing the Brokenhearted."

Joyce's "Mind Package" features five different audio tape series on the subject of the mind. They include: "Mental Strongholds and Mindsets"; "Wilderness Mentality"; "The Mind of the Flesh"; "The Wandering, Wondering Mind"; and "Mind, Mouth, Moods & Attitudes." The package also contains Joyce's powerful 260-page book, *Battlefield of the Mind*. On the subject of love she has two tape series entitled, "Love Is..." and "Love: The Ultimate Power."

Write to Joyce Meyer's office for a resource catalog and further information on how to obtain the tapes you need to bring total healing to your life.

To contact the author write:

Joyce Meyer
Life In The Word, Inc.
P. O. Box 655
Fenton, Missouri 63026
or call:
(314) 349-0303

Please include your testimony
or help received from this
book when you write.
Your prayer requests are welcome.

In Canada, please write:
Joyce Meyer Ministries Canada, Inc.
P. O. Box 2995
London, ON N6A 4H9

In Australia, please write:
Joyce Meyer Ministries-Australia
Locked Bag 77
Mansfield Delivery Centre
Queensland 4122
or call:
(07) 3349 1200

Books by Joyce Meyer

Life in the Word Devotional

Be Anxious for Nothing—
The Art of Casting Your Cares
and Resting in God

The *Help Me!* Series:
I'm Stressed!
I'm Insecure!
I'm Discouraged!
I'm Depressed!
I'm Worried!
I'm Afraid!

Don't Dread — Overcoming the Spirit of Dread
With the Supernatural Power of God

Managing Your Emotions
Instead of Your Emotions Managing You

Life in the Word

Healing the Brokenhearted

"Me and My Big Mouth!"

Prepare To Prosper

Do It! Afraid

*Expect a Move of God in Your Life...**Suddenly***

Enjoying Where You Are On the Way
to Where You Are Going

The Most Important Decision You'll Ever Make

When, God, When?

Why, God, Why?

The Word, The Name, The Blood

Battlefield of the Mind

Tell Them I Love Them

Peace

The Root of Rejection

Beauty for Ashes

If Not for the Grace of God

By Dave Meyer
Nuggets of Life

Available from your local bookstore.

Harrison House
Tulsa, Oklahoma 74153

The Harrison House Vision

Proclaiming the truth and the power
Of the Gospel of Jesus Christ
With excellence;

Challenging Christians to
Live victoriously,
Grow spiritually,
Know God intimately.